Keep Yourself Safe on the Internet

Avoiding Dangerous Downloads

Karen McMichael

PowerKiDS press.

NEW YORK

Published in 2018 by The Rosen Publishing Group, Inc.
29 East 21st Street, New York, NY 10010

Editor: Kate Mikoley
Book Design: Rachel Rising
Interior Layout: Michael Flynn

Photo Credits: Cover Johner Images/Getty Images; cover, pp. 3–4, 6, 8, 10, 12, 14, 16, 18, 20, 22–24 (background) Creative Mood/
Shutterstock.com; p. 5 Tomsickova Tatyana/Shutterstock.com; p. 7 quavondo/E+/Getty Images; p. 9 Stuart Jenner/Shutterstock.com;
pp. 11, 22 Rawpixel.com/Shutterstock.com; p. 13 danchooalex/E+/Getty Images; p. 15 Here/Shutterstock.com; pp. 17, 21 wavebreakmedia/
Shutterstock.com; p. 18 Mile Atanasov/Shutterstock.com; p. 19 goodluz/Shutterstock.com.

Cataloging-in-Publication Data

Names: McMichael, Karen.
Title: Avoiding dangerous downloads / Karen McMichael.
Description: New York : PowerKids Press, 2018. | Series: Keep yourself safe on the Internet | Includes index.
Identifiers: ISBN 9781538325711 (pbk.) | ISBN 9781538324998 (library bound) | ISBN 9781538325728 (6 pack)
Subjects: LCSH: Internet--Security measures--Juvenile literature. | Computer security--Juvenile literature. | Computer network resources--
Evaluation--Juvenile literature.
Classification: LCC TK5105.875.I57 M36 2018 | DDC 004.678--dc23

Manufactured in China

CPSIA Compliance Information: Batch #BW18PK For further information contact Rosen Publishing, New York, New York at 1-800-237-9932.

Contents

Downloading Dangers. 4

Issues with E-mails 10

Find Safe Websites 14

Glossary .23

Index 24

Websites .24

Downloading Dangers

Going online is fun! You can **download** games, music, and movies. You have to be careful, though. Some things are safe to download, but others may be dangerous, or unsafe.

5

Some downloads may carry a **virus**. A computer virus is like an illness for your computer! You can spread a virus to your friends' computers without even knowing it.

7

Some files look safe, but are actually viruses. Ask an adult before you download anything. They can help figure out if it's safe.

Issues with E-mails

E-mails may be dangerous, too. Be careful if you get an e-mail from someone you don't know. Don't open **attachments** from people you don't know.

When you're online, don't talk to people you don't know. People you don't know are called strangers. Never tell a stranger anything **private**. Your full name, address, and phone number are private.

13

Find Safe Websites

Be careful using websites you don't know well. They might look safe, but they could be bad. If you're not sure about something, don't download it.

15

If you want to use a new website, have an adult check it first. They'll be able to tell if it's safe or if it might harm your computer.

Some computer programs can stop computer viruses. Your parents or teachers can put these programs on your computer. Still, be careful. Some viruses and problems can get through.

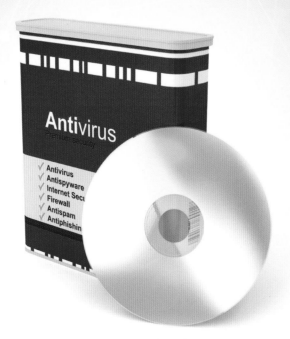

19

Sometimes mistakes happen. If you download something you shouldn't have, tell an adult right away. They might be able to fix the problem before it gets worse. They will be glad you told them.

21

Some downloads are great, but others can be dangerous. Always make sure something is safe before downloading it. That's a sure way to keep yourself safe on the Internet!

Glossary

attachment: A file included in an e-mail.

download: To copy information to your computer from somewhere else, usually over the Internet. Also, something that has been downloaded.

private: Information not meant for other people to know.

virus: A computer program that harms your computer.

Index

A
adult, 8, 16, 20
attachments, 10

C
computer, 6, 16, 18

E
e-mails, 10

F
files, 8

G
games, 4

M
movies, 4
music, 4

P
programs, 18

S
strangers, 12

V
virus, 6, 8, 18

W
websites, 14, 16

Websites

Due to the changing nature of Internet links, PowerKids Press has developed an online list of websites related to the subject of this book. This site is updated regularly. Please use this link to access the list: www.powerkidslinks.com/kysi/add